SRA®
MULTIPLE SKILLS
SERIES: Reading

Third Edition

Richard A. Boning

SRA
McGraw-Hill

Columbus, Ohio

A Division of The McGraw·Hill Companies

Cover, Christopher Arnesen/Tony Stone Images

SRA/McGraw-Hill

A Division of The **McGraw·Hill** *Companies*

Printed in the United States of America.

Send all inquiries to:
SRA/McGraw-Hill
250 Old Wilson Bridge Road
Suite 310
Worthington, Ohio 43085

ISBN 0-02-688426-7

 2 3 4 5 6 7 8 9 SCG 02 01 00 99 98

To the Teacher

PURPOSE

The *Multiple Skills Series* is a nonconsumable reading program designed to develop a cluster of key reading skills and to integrate these skills with each other and with the other language arts. *Multiple Skills* is also diagnostic, making it possible for you to identify specific types of reading skills that might be causing difficulty for individual students.

FOR WHOM

The twelve levels of the *Multiple Skills Series* are geared to students who comprehend on the pre-first- through ninth-grade reading levels.

- The Picture Level is for children who have not acquired a basic sight vocabulary.
- The Preparatory 1 Level is for children who have developed a limited basic sight vocabulary.
- The Preparatory 2 Level is for children who have a basic sight vocabulary but are not yet reading on the first-grade level.
- Books A through I are appropriate for students who can read on grade levels one through nine respectively. Because of their high interest level, the books may also be used effectively with students functioning at these levels of competence in other grades.

The **Multiple Skills Series Placement Tests** will help you determine the appropriate level for each student.

PLACEMENT TESTS

The Elementary Placement Test (for grades Pre-1 through 3) and the Midway Placement Tests (for grades 4–9) will help you place each student properly. The tests consist of representative units selected from the series. The test books contain two forms, X and Y. One form may be used for placement and the second as a posttest to measure progress. The tests are easy to administer and score. Blackline Masters are provided for worksheets and student performance profiles.

THE BOOKS

This third edition of the *Multiple Skills Series* maintains the quality and focus that have distinguished this program for over 25 years. The series includes four books at each level, Picture Level through Level I. Each book in the Picture Level through Level B contains 25 units. Each book in Level C through Level I contains 50 units. The units within each book increase in difficulty. The books within a level also increase in difficulty—Level A, Book 2 is slightly more difficult than Level A, Book 1, and so on. This gradual increase in difficulty permits students to advance from one book to the next and from one level to the next without frustration.

Each book contains an **About This Book** page, which explains the skills to the students and shows them how to approach reading the selections and questions. In the lowest levels, you should read About This Book to the children.

The questions that follow each unit are designed to develop specific reading skills. In the lowest levels, you should read the questions to the children.

In Level E, the question pattern in each unit is
1. Title (main idea)
2. Stated detail
3. Stated detail
4. Inference or conclusion
5. Vocabulary

The **Language Activity Pages** (LAP) in each level consist of four parts: Exercising Your Skill, Expanding Your Skill, Exploring Language, and Expressing Yourself. These pages lead the students beyond the book through a broadening spiral of writing, speaking, and other individual and group language activities that apply, extend, and integrate the skills being developed. You may use all, some, or none of the activities in any LAP; however, some LAP activities depend on preceding ones. In the lowest levels, you should read the LAPs to the children.

In Levels C-I, each set of Language Activity Pages focuses on a particular skill developed through the book. Emphasis progresses from the most concrete to the most abstract:

First LAP	Details
Second LAP	Vocabulary
Third LAP	Main ideas
Last LAP	Inferences and conclusions

SESSIONS

The *Multiple Skills Series* is basically an individualized reading program that may be used with small groups or an entire class. Short sessions are the most effective. Use a short session every day or every other day, completing a few units in each session. Time allocated to the Language Activity Pages depends on the abilities of the individual students.

SCORING

Students should record their answers on the reproducible worksheets. The worksheets make scoring easier and provide uniform records of the children's work. Using worksheets also avoids consuming the books.

Because it is important for the students to know how they are progressing, you should score the units as soon as they've been completed. Then you can discuss the questions and activities with the students and encourage them to justify their responses. Many of the LAPs are open-ended and do not lend themselves to an objective score; for this reason, there are no answer keys for these pages.

A careful reader thinks about the writer's words and pays attention to what the story or article is mainly about. A careful reader also "reads between the lines" because a writer does not tell the reader everything. A careful reader tries to figure out the meaning of new words too. As you read the stories and articles in this book, you will practice all of these reading skills.

First you will read a story and choose a good title for it. The title will tell something about the **main idea** of the article or story. To choose a good title, you must know what the story or article is mainly about.

The next two questions will ask you about facts that are stated in the story or article. To answer these questions, read carefully. Pay attention to the **details.**

The fourth question will ask you to figure out **something the writer doesn't tell you directly.** For example, you might read that Dr. Fujihara received an emergency call, drove to Elm Street, and rushed into a house. Even though the writer doesn't tell you directly, you can figure out that Dr. Fujihara knows how to drive and that someone in the house is probably sick. You use the information the author provides plus your own knowledge and experience to figure out what is probably true.

The last question will ask you to tell the meaning of a word in the story or article. You can figure out what the word means by studying its **context**—the other words and sentences in the story. Read the following sentences.

> Clara ran out to the garden excitedly. Vegetables were growing in neat rows in the small, raised beds. Each bed was surrounded by flowers. Clara was not interested in the vegetables. She wanted to see the daisies and the bright yellow *marigolds.*

Did you figure out that marigolds are flowers? What clues in the story helped you figure this out?

This book will help you practice your reading skills. As you learn to use all of these skills together, you will become a better reader.

When most people think of Helen Keller, they can't help but think of Anne Sullivan. Helen, the star pupil, and Anne, the model teacher, go together like a hand and glove. Both of these women were truly remarkable.

Helen Keller was left deaf and blind from an illness when she was a baby. Anne Sullivan, nearly blind herself, taught Helen to read Braille, a system of raised dots designed for the blind. She also taught her to "talk" with her fingers. Using these tools to overcome her *handicaps*, Helen developed her keen mind. She received many honors for her books and other works.

When Anne Sullivan was near death, someone said to her, "Teacher, you must get well. Without you, Helen would be nothing." Anne replied, "That would mean that I have failed." Do you agree?

1. The best title is—
   (A) Helen Keller
   (B) Anne Sullivan
   (C) Model Teacher and Star Pupil
   (D) Two Friends

2. Helen Keller became deaf and blind from—
   (A) birth   (B) an accident
   (C) an illness   (D) adulthood

3. Anne Sullivan was Helen's—
   (A) relative   (B) nurse
   (C) pupil   (D) teacher

4. When it comes to these two women—
   (A) both failed   (B) neither was famous
   (C) neither failed   (D) both gave up

5. The word "handicaps" in line nine means—
   (A) enemies   (B) poor grades
   (C) physical challenges (D) health habits

Although herring gulls are called "sea gulls," they live near lakes, ponds, streams, and rivers. They are not often found far out at sea. Sometimes they follow ships in open waters, looking for food that people throw overboard.

It is easy to spot gulls. They have gray wings that are tipped with black, yellow beaks, and large, white bodies. You can tell them by their cry, a lonely kee-ow—kee-ow, as well as by their graceful flight patterns.

Most of the time, gulls will *remain* around harbors looking for food. They will eat almost anything dead or alive. Not only do they bring beauty to the coast, but they also help to keep the waterfront clean.

---

1. The best title is—
   (A) Following Ships
   (B) What Sea Gulls Are Like
   (C) Bringing Beauty to the Coast
   (D) What Sea Gulls Eat

2. Gulls follow ships, looking for—
   (A) people   (B) food
   (C) other gulls   (D) the shore

3. The story says that the gull's body is—
   (A) small   (B) white
   (C) green   (D) red

4. When it comes to food, gulls are—
   (A) not choosy   (B) very fussy
   (C) not interested   (D) foolish

5. The word "remain" in line nine means—
   (A) build nests   (B) avoid
   (C) stay   (D) swim

This was a toy fair without equal. On this February day, 18,000 buyers had come from no less than 74 countries. The toymakers themselves numbered over 1,000. Reporters from magazines, newspapers, television, and radio were there too—over 600 of them. They were all in New York for the 95th yearly American International Toy Fair, but the real stars of the *exhibition* were the thousands of new games, dolls, toys, and stuffed animals. They would soon find their way to stores around the world in 1998.

Yet, some important people were missing. Guess who wasn't invited? The rules for the toy fair stated that only people over the age of 14 were welcome!

1. The best title is—
   (A) Time to Buy Toys
   (B) Reporters at the Toy Fair
   (C) Toy Fair Without Equal
   (D) Rules for the Toy Fair

2. The toy buyers came from—
   (A) 18 countries
   (B) 74 countries
   (C) 600 countries
   (D) New York

3. The toy fair was held in—
   (A) different countries
   (B) October
   (C) New York
   (D) 1990

4. You can tell that the author thinks the toy fair should have included—
   (A) fewer reporters
   (B) more toy makers
   (C) live animals
   (D) children

5. The word "exhibition" in line six means—
   (A) city
   (B) store
   (C) display
   (D) sky

If someone is bashful, it means the person does not like to be seen or noticed. Do you know what the most bashful bird in the world is? It is the spiny babbler.

Spiny babblers were first seen in the country of Nepal in the 1840s. Then they were not seen again. Scientists thought they had become *extinct*. It was not until 1948 that the next spiny babbler was seen—over one hundred years later! Since then, a number of them have been seen, but only for a minute. They quickly dart away.

Don't you think everyone would agree that the spiny babbler is the most bashful bird in the world?

---

1. The best title is—
    (A) The Birds of Nepal
    (B) The Spiny Babbler—A Bashful Bird
    (C) The Spiny Babbler—A High Flier
    (D) Scientists Study Birds

2. The spiny babbler was not seen for over—
    (A) 50 years   (B) 10,000 years
    (C) 100 years   (D) 1,000 years

3. The story says that the spiny babbler doesn't like to be—
    (A) eaten   (B) caught
    (C) seen   (D) heard

4. The story suggests that today there are—
    (A) no more spiny babblers   (B) still a number of spiny babblers
    (C) millions of spiny babblers (D) too many spiny babblers

5. The word "extinct" in line six means—
    (A) no longer existing   (B) too many
    (C) very sleepy   (D) very thin

A baby girl was born in Illinois in 1860. Her name was Jane Addams. She grew up to be a great worker for the poor.

When she was six, Jane saw the homes of some poor people. She said some day she'd build a big house and invite the poor to live there.

In 1889 she found a dirty brick house in Chicago. It was a *mansion* that had been built by a Mr. Hull. Jane cleaned it from top to bottom. Then she opened it to the poor. Whole families came—to learn English, to cook and sew, and to get free baths! Although Jane Addams died in 1935, the work she started in Hull House goes on today. Now all kinds of people are helped through health and child-care centers and other Hull House service groups.

---

1. The best title is—
   (A) The Homes of Poor People
   (B) Jane Addams Helps the Poor
   (C) Jane Addams Cleans a House
   (D) Learning to Cook and Sew

2. Jane Addams was born in—
   (A) 1935   (B) 1835
   (C) 1860   (D) 1889

3. Hull House was made of—
   (A) brick   (B) wood
   (C) glass   (D) stone

4. You can tell that Hull House was—
   (A) very small   (B) very large
   (C) without a kitchen   (D) without a bathroom

5. The word "mansion" in line seven means—
   (A) large house   (B) small house
   (C) apartment   (D) park

Many cities have smog. Smog is smoke and fog *combined*. It is bad for people's health. One city that does not have any smog is Reykjavik, Iceland.

Reykjavik does not have smog because it has very little smoke. In Reykjavik, most homes, offices, and factories do not have to burn things to get heat. They use the steam and hot water from the city's many hot springs. The water from these hot springs is piped to buildings, swimming pools, and even to farms to keep the plants warm.

Reykjavik is not only a beautiful city—it is also a healthy city.

1. The best title is—
   (A) Smog and Sickness
   (B) Heating Homes and Factories
   (C) A Trip to Reykjavik, Iceland
   (D) Reykjavik—A Healthy City

2. Smog is—
   (A) fog and mist   (B) smoke and mist
   (C) smoke and fog   (D) steam and fog

3. Water from the hot springs is carried—
   (A) in large tank trucks   (B) through pipes
   (C) in huge pails   (D) by ditches

4. The story does *not* say the hot water is used for—
   (A) swimming   (B) farming
   (C) filling fountains   (D) heating homes

5. The word "combined" in line one means—
   (A) separated   (B) mixed
   (C) heated   (D) destroyed

UNIT 7

Years ago a courageous man named Charles Zimmy made records as a long-distance swimmer. After much training, he set a record when he swam for eighty-one hours without stopping. Then, in Hawaii, he broke his own record by swimming for one hundred hours straight.

Zimmy's greatest feat was swimming the Hudson River from Albany to New York City. The distance between these cities is 147 miles!

Perhaps no one will ever *match* these records. They certainly are amazing, especially when we consider his great handicap. Charles Zimmy had no legs.

---

1. The best title is—
   (A) Zimmy Goes to Hawaii
   (B) Zimmy, the Amazing Long-distance Swimmer
   (C) Zimmy Swims the Hudson River
   (D) Swimming Against the Tide

2. Charles Zimmy swam from Albany to—
   (A) Boston   (B) Syracuse
   (C) New York City   (D) Buffalo

3. According to the story, Charles Zimmy had—
   (A) little strength   (B) great courage
   (C) many friends   (D) a smooth stroke

4. In Hawaii, Zimmy broke his old record by—
   (A) 1 hour   (B) 19 hours
   (C) 5 hours   (D) 40 hours

5. The word "match" in line nine means—
   (A) find   (B) strike
   (C) equal   (D) light

Everyone knows that a farm is a place where food is grown. We have all seen pictures of fields of grain and of cows grazing in a pasture. But have you ever heard of a farm on the bottom of the ocean? There are such farms. These farms raise oysters, a popular food in the United States. An oyster is a small sea animal that lives in a shell. Its meat is delicious.

Many years ago there were a great many oysters. Then factories began emptying *waste* materials into the ocean and many oysters died. People also started eating more oysters. The government studied the problem and put controls on factories. It also helped people begin "oyster farms," where millions of oysters are now grown every year.

1. The best title is—
   (A) Good-bye, Oysters
   (B) Fields of Grain
   (C) Oyster Farms
   (D) Animal in a Shell

2. Oyster farms are found in the—
   (A) fields   (B) ocean
   (C) factories   (D) country

3. Oyster farms were helped by the—
   (A) government   (B) factories
   (C) fish   (D) waste materials

4. You can tell that most farms are—
   (A) in factories   (B) in others countries
   (C) on the land   (D) on the ocean floor

5. The word "waste" in line eight means—
   (A) important   (B) not used
   (C) helpful   (D) necessary

Can you sing? Amy Beach could sing songs when she was only one year old!

At age four, Amy wrote music for dancing. She started piano lessons at six. In Boston, in 1883, Amy gave her first public performance playing the piano. She was sixteen.

As Amy aged, she wrote more music. She *composed* music for orchestras, churches, opera singers, and singing groups. She composed over 150 pieces of music. She also helped other composers. Amy Beach was the most famous American woman composer of her time.

1. The best title is—
   (A) Amy Beach—Dancer
   (B) Playing the Piano
   (C) Amy Beach—Composer
   (D) The Boston Concert

2. Amy could sing songs at age—
   (A) fifteen   (B) one
   (C) five   (D) sixteen

3. Amy gave her first public performance in—
   (A) England   (B) her parents' house
   (C) Boston   (D) her school

4. The story does *not* tell—
   (A) when Amy began piano   (B) when Amy began to sing
       lessons
   (C) if Amy helped others   (D) when Amy died

5. The word "composed" in line six means—
   (A) danced to music   (B) wrote music
   (C) hummed music   (D) listened to music

The coldest and most difficult place in the world in which to live is Antarctica. Antarctica is the land of snow and ice near the South Pole. Most people do not think there is much life in the icy waters around it. They are wrong.

Antarctica's seas are full of life. There are many kinds of fish, water birds, seals, and whales. They eat the thick plant life in the sea and the smaller water animals. Some whales, for example, eat more than a ton of food every day.

The most famous animal of Antarctica is the penguin. It *struts* around the icy beaches as if it were a movie star walking down the street.

1. The best title is—
   (A) Thick Plant Life
   (B) Life Around Antarctica
   (C) Tons of Food
   (D) Penguins

2. The most famous animal of Antarctica is the—
   (A) whale   (B) seal
   (C) penguin   (D) fox

3. Antarctica has—
   (A) much ice   (B) warm weather
   (C) flocks of geese (D) warm water

4. Around Antarctica there—
   (A) are many people   (B) is little plant life
   (C) are many animals (D) is little snow

5. The word "struts" in line nine means—
   (A) swims gracefully (B) walks proudly
   (C) runs swiftly   (D) jumps happily

Thomas A. Edison was a great inventor. One day, about one hundred years ago, Edison stood by a strange-looking machine. He said the words, "Mary had a little lamb." Then something *marvelous* happened—the machine talked back. He had invented the phonograph.

At first the machine did not work very well. Another famous inventor, Alexander Graham Bell, helped Edison to improve it. Still people were not sure that they liked listening to the phonograph. Then a great singer, Enrico Caruso, made some records. Everyone loved them, and the phonograph became popular.

Today we can listen to our favorite singers whenever we want to—thanks to Thomas A. Edison.

1. The best title is—
   (A) Alexander Graham Bell
   (B) How Enrico Caruso Made Records
   (C) The Invention of the Phonograph
   (D) Listening to Singers

2. The name of a great singer was—
   (A) Thomas A. Edison
   (B) Alexander Graham Bell
   (C) Enrico Caruso
   (D) Mary Lamb

3. Edison called his "talking machine" the—
   (A) photograph
   (B) telephone
   (C) telegraph
   (D) phonograph

4. Sometimes even a great inventor needs—
   (A) some help
   (B) less time
   (C) our thanks
   (D) more money

5. The word "marvelous" in line three means—
   (A) expected
   (B) wonderful
   (C) terrible
   (D) regular

Diving is an exciting sport. It is thrilling to watch a diver fly from a high place to the water below. Some dives, however, can be dangerous. Possibly the most dangerous dive in the world takes place every day in Acapulco, Mexico.

Acapulco is a place that many people like to visit. One thing they all want to see is the high dive that young Mexicans take from the top of a cliff. The Mexicans, all specially trained for this dive, climb the cliff. Everyone watches as they get ready to dive. Down they plunge—118 feet into only twelve feet of water. The divers enter the water at sixty miles per hour!

No wonder *tourists* come from around the world to watch the famous high dive in Acapulco.

---

1. The best title is—
   (A) Acapulco and Its Visitors
   (B) The High Dive at Acapulco
   (C) Mexicans Watch the Dive
   (D) Learning to Dive Well

2. The Mexican divers in the story are—
   (A) old   (B) trained
   (C) afraid   (D) often hurt

3. The divers in Acapulco dive—
   (A) once a week   (B) twice a week
   (C) on Sunday only   (D) every day

4. Visitors enjoy the diving in Acapulco because it is—
   (A) not dangerous   (B) free
   (C) thrilling   (D) funny

5. The word "tourists" in line eleven means—
   (A) Mexicans   (B) visitors
   (C) divers   (D) Americans

A. Exercising Your Skill

In Unit 11, you read that Alexander Graham Bell improved Thomas Edison's phonograph. You may also know that Bell invented the telephone. Bell, however, didn't try to invent the telephone. It happened rather by accident. Bell's mother and sister were deaf. He was trying to invent a machine to make sound louder so that they could hear. Other inventions have also happened somewhat by accident. Read this passage.

> Penicillin is a wonder drug. It kills about ninety different kinds of bacteria, or germs. Over the years penicillin has saved millions and millions of lives.
>
> Alexander Fleming invented penicillin. But he invented it quite by accident. Fleming was a scientist at a hospital in London. One day in 1928, he was working on an experiment. He was growing some bacteria in a small dish. That night his helper forgot to cover the dish. During the night some mold blew in the open window and fell on the dish. When Fleming came in the next morning, the bacteria were dead. He discovered the mold and called it penicillin.

Does effort over a long period of time produce most inventions? Thomas Edison once said, "Invention is one percent inspiration and ninety-nine percent perspiration." Discuss what this means with your class. Do you agree with Edison, or do you think accidents probably produce most inventions?

Take one side of this argument. List reasons to support your side. Ask your teacher to write everyone's reasons in two separate columns on the board. Discuss the reasons. Which side has the most good reasons?

B. Expanding Your Skill

What other inventions would you like to know about? Choose one of the following inventions, or choose one on your own. Then find a book in the library that tells about that invention. On a piece of paper, write how that invention got started. Be ready to tell your classmates about the invention you chose.

roller skates	drinking straws	blue jeans
ballpoint pens	zippers	the game of basketball

C. Exploring Language

Have you ever thought about something that needs to be invented? For example, have you ever gone out into the rain with your hands full? Maybe someone should invent an umbrella that doesn't have to be held. To get an idea for an invention, think about these questions.

1. What do you own now that could be made better?
2. What would make your life better or easier?
3. What would make the lives of your family better or easier?
4. Do you have a problem? What would solve it?

Make a list of two or three possible inventions. Give each invention a name. You also may want to draw a picture of each one. Then briefly explain why each one would be a good invention.

D. Expressing Yourself

Choose one of these activities.

1. Read about the personal life of Thomas Edison. You will find many interesting facts. For example, at the age of twelve, he started his own business. At sixteen he became an inventor. When you have finished, write a diary entry. Write it as if *you* were Thomas Edison. In the entry explain one event in his personal life, but use the pronouns *I, me,* and *my.* Include important facts and details to make the diary entry seem real.

2. Thomas Edison died at eighty-four. At that time he held 1,093 patents. A patent is an agreement between an inventor and the United States government. An inventor agrees to tell all about his or her invention. In return, the government does not allow anyone else to use the same invention for a while. For more information about patents, write a letter to: Superintendent of Documents, U.S. Government Printing Office, Washington, D.C. 20402, and ask for a copy of *The Story of the United States Patent Office.* Then make a list of the most important facts in it. Share what you have learned with your classmates.

There is one song that you probably sing several times a year. You may not know it by its 1893 title "Good Morning to All."

The song was written by two sisters from Louisville, Kentucky. Mildred Hill, a teacher, wrote the music, and her sister, Patty Hill, a school principal, wrote the words. They never meant for it to be sung at birthday celebrations. The sisters used the song to welcome young children to the classroom in the morning.

In 1924, Robert H. Coleman, a *publisher,* changed all that. He included the Hills' song in one of his songbooks. He also changed one of the lines of the song to read "Happy birthday to you." By 1933, the Hills' song had become popular and was known by its unofficial "Happy Birthday to You" title.

---

1. The best title is—
    (A) Two Musical Sisters
    (B) A School Song Becomes a Birthday Song
    (C) Robert H. Coleman: Song Publisher
    (D) "Good Morning to All"

2. "Happy Birthday to You" was known by that title by—
    (A) 1893   (B) 1924
    (C) 1833   (D) 1933

3. Patty Hill wrote—
    (A) the music   (B) the words and music
    (C) the words   (D) a songbook

4. You can tell from the story that Coleman—
    (A) didn't like music   (B) liked to sing
    (C) made the song popular   (D) hurt the song

5. The word "publisher" in line eight means—
    (A) producer of books   (B) owner of books
    (C) singer of songs   (D) reader of books

UNIT 14

Are your plants growing as well as you think they should? If not, maybe some music will help.

The idea may sound crazy, but some scientists say it is true. Music "excites" the cells of plants and they grow faster. Any *type* of music will help, but the best kind is played by a flute or violin.

These scientists do not know exactly why plants grow better with music. They do believe, however, that it works. They have taken two groups of plants and played music to only one group. That group grows greener, stronger, and has more roots.

If your plants look weak, try a little music. It may work!

---

1. The best title is—
   (A) Music and Growing Plants
   (B) Flutes and Violins
   (C) Two Groups of Plants
   (D) Growing Stronger Roots

2. Some scientists say that music excites the—
   (A) roots of plants   (B) leaves of plants
   (C) cells of plants   (D) large trees

3. The story says that music helps plants to grow—
   (A) smaller   (B) better fruit
   (C) greener   (D) slower

4. Most plants would probably do well with—
   (A) all music   (B) rock music
   (C) loud music   (D) soothing music

5. The word "type" in line four means—
   (A) note   (B) dance
   (C) kind   (D) sound

An explorer named Juan Ponce de León became friendly with American Indians. They told him of a pool of water that kept people young. Ponce de León became excited. He went searching for the "fountain of youth." He never found it.

Many people now believe that the pool of water must have been a hot spring. There are many hot springs that have minerals in the water. They make you feel relaxed. Doctors are not sure if the hot springs *improve* your health, but they do make you feel better.

One thing is certain. Hot springs do not keep you young. Ponce de León grew old while looking for a place to stay young.

---

1. The best title is—
    (A) American Indians Help Ponce de León
    (B) Searching for Youth
    (C) Growing Old
    (D) The Hot Springs of America

2. Ponce de León wanted to—
    (A) grow old   (B) become relaxed
    (C) stay young   (D) cure a cold

3. Ponce de León learned of the "fountain of youth" from—
    (A) doctors   (B) American Indians
    (C) children   (D) enemies

4. Bathing in a hot spring would be—
    (A) terrible   (B) enjoyable
    (C) dangerous   (D) impossible

5. The word "improve" in line eight means—
    (A) make young   (B) make worse
    (C) make better   (D) make old

A motel is a hotel where people traveling by car can stop for the night. The word "motel" comes from two words—"motor" and "hotel." The word itself was *coined* in 1924.

"Hotel" and "motel" are just two of the words that name a place where travelers can spend the night. Long ago, George Washington used to stop at inns. He often complained of bugs and thin bear blankets. Wouldn't he be pleased with the beautiful motels of today?

Today there are many kinds of "hotels." There are "boatels," where you can dock a boat; "airtels," for those traveling by small airplanes; and "horsetels," for people riding horses. How times have changed!

1. The best title is—
    (A) Different Kinds of "Hotels"
    (B) George Washington Slept Here
    (C) Motels of Long Ago
    (D) Traveling by Boat

2. "Airtels" are for people who travel by—
    (A) car   (B) airplane
    (C) boat   (D) horse

3. The story says that George Washington complained about the—
    (A) food   (B) blankets
    (C) television   (D) noise

4. The story suggests that there is a kind of hotel for—
    (A) every pet   (B) people who like pets
    (C) every person   (D) people who like to complain

5. The word "coined" in line three means—
    (A) invented   (B) forgotten
    (C) lost   (D) missed

The yarn spinners who flock to Jonesborough, Tennessee, each October are weavers of stories. Of the more than sixty storytelling festivals nationwide, the National Storytelling Festival in Jonesborough is the oldest and largest. It was founded in 1973, when people who shared the joy of storytelling gathered together from nearby towns and states. They were farmers, teachers, and singers. Everyone had such a good time that they continued the tradition each year.

Everyone is invited to *swap* a story at the "Swappin' Ground." The stories that are exchanged are as different as the ways in which they are told. At the Old Jonesborough Cemetery on Saturday night, the yarn spinners tell ghost stories. Shivers and shudders!

1. The best title is—
   - (A) 1973—a Great Year
   - (B) Sixty Storytelling Festivals
   - (C) Yarn Spinners in Jonesborough
   - (D) A Cemetery Full of Ghosts

2. Jonesborough is in—
   - (A) Tennessee
   - (B) Iowa
   - (C) Arkansas
   - (D) California

3. The people who gathered in 1973 included farmers and—
   - (A) salespersons
   - (B) teachers
   - (C) factory workers
   - (D) doctors

4. You can tell that an important reason for going to the festival is to—
   - (A) weave colored cloth
   - (B) hear new stories
   - (C) visit cemeteries
   - (D) see ghosts

5. The word "swap" in line nine means—
   - (A) buy
   - (B) trade
   - (C) sell
   - (D) borrow

Fairbanks, Alaska, is a busy city today. Few people know that if it were not for two thousand pounds of bacon, the city would not be there!

It was in 1906 that a small fire started in the office of the town dentist. Soon it spread, and everyone in Fairbanks began fighting it. Hoses were connected but little water was shooting out. A wood-burning furnace was being used to keep up the water *pressure*. But soon the supply of wood had run out, and the stream of water became a trickle. Then someone had an idea. If there wasn't any wood, why not use the ton of bacon stored in a warehouse? As the bacon was thrown on the fire, the heat from the hot grease rapidly built up the water pressure. Water came pouring from the hoses. The city of Fairbanks was saved.

1. The best title is—
   (A) Lost Water Pressure
   (B) Fairbanks, Alaska
   (C) Fighting Fires
   (D) Bacon Saves a City

2. The fire started in a—
   (A) warehouse   (B) dentist's office
   (C) barn   (D) forest

3. Today Fairbanks is—
   (A) busy   (B) destroyed
   (C) on fire   (D) selling bacon

4. Fairbanks was in danger because there was no—
   (A) bacon   (B) fire
   (C) wood   (D) help

5. The word "pressure" in line seven means—
   (A) hose   (B) force
   (C) start   (D) loss

If you like nuts, you might like to visit the Nut Museum. It may sound a little nutty, but there actually is a museum of nuts. It's in a big house in Old Lyme, Connecticut.

Inside, you'll find displays of all kinds of nuts, including some kinds you can't eat. There are paintings of nuts and a lot of different nutcrackers from all parts of the world. On the lawn outside the museum are—of course—nut trees.

How much does it cost to go into this museum? The *admission* is a small fee of money and one nut—any kind.

---

1. The best title is—
   (A) Growing Nuts
   (B) A Nut Museum
   (C) A Beautiful Lawn
   (D) Spending Money

2. The museum in the story is in a—
   (A) small house   (B) tall tower
   (C) big house   (D) large park

3. On the lawn outside the museum are—
   (A) large signs   (B) nut trees
   (C) many benches   (D) small holes

4. The story does *not* tell—
   (A) where the museum is   (B) if there is a fee to get in
   (C) how many nuts are   (D) if there are paintings
       displayed

5. The word "admission" in line eight means—
   (A) price to enter   (B) chance to see
   (C) price to leave   (D) right to borrow

The liveliest spot to be on New Year's Day just might be Pasadena, California. Each year about two million people *assemble* there to watch a flower festival. This yearly event—the Parade of Roses—began in 1890. Some experts boast that it now draws the largest crowd in America. Each year the event gets bigger and better. The attraction can be seen along the eight-mile parade route. Wide-eyed tourists watch as one large, colorful float of flowers after another passes by. The marching bands are favorites, too.

Then, on New Year's afternoon, Pasadena also hosts the Rose Bowl football game. The game is played between two champion college teams. So if you don't have plans for New Year's Day, and you like crowds, flowers, and football, head for Pasadena.

1. The best title is—
   (A) New Year's Day in Pasadena
   (B) Roses in Bloom
   (C) The Rose Bowl
   (D) Heading for Pasadena

2. The Parade of Roses is—
   (A) a New Year's Eve event   (B) a football game
   (C) a music festival   (D) a yearly event

3. The football game at the Rose Bowl is played by—
   (A) professionals   (B) college students
   (C) paraders   (D) high-school students

4. The tourists probably most enjoy the—
   (A) crowds   (B) weather
   (C) excitement   (D) bands

5. The word "assemble" in line two means—
   (A) march   (B) gather
   (C) fly   (D) leave

To find the largest monument to American Presidents, you would have to travel to the Black Hills of South Dakota. There, on Mount Rushmore, the carved faces of four U. S. Presidents—Washington, Jefferson, Lincoln, and Theodore Roosevelt—can be seen for sixty-one miles.

The faces were carved by the *sculptor* Gutzon Borglum, with the help of his son. The project was begun in 1927. Borglum spent fourteen years carving the faces. When he died, his son completed the face of Lincoln.

Borglum did not do things on a small scale. The face of Washington, for example, is sixty feet high! Imagine coming face-to-face with this great American!

---

1. The best title is—
   (A) Gutzon Borglum and Son
   (B) A Monument to Four Great Presidents
   (C) Face to Face
   (D) The Faces of Washington and Lincoln

2. The Mount Rushmore monument does *not* include the carved face of—
   (A) Franklin Roosevelt   (B) George Washington
   (C) Abraham Lincoln   (D) Thomas Jefferson

3. The faces on Mount Rushmore are all—
   (A) artists   (B) U. S. Presidents
   (C) women   (D) American Indians

4. You can tell that all the carved faces are—
   (A) handsome   (B) young
   (C) huge   (D) small

5. The word "sculptor" in line six means—
   (A) artist who paints   (B) artist who makes statues
   (C) artist's assistant   (D) artist's model

The world's tallest tree is a giant redwood. Growing in California, this redwood is 367 feet high—almost three times taller than the Statue of Liberty. It grows in a thick forest and was *discovered* in 1963!

At one time there were redwood trees covering over two million acres. Then they began to be destroyed by wind, lightning, floods, and by people cutting them down. This caused the government to make the area a national park. This means that no one can cut down the redwoods. There are also forest rangers in the park to care for them. The national park is 500 miles long.

Visitors will now be able to enjoy the giant redwoods more, knowing that the trees are being protected.

---

1. The best title is—
    (A) The Trees of California
    (B) The Giant Redwoods
    (C) Redwood Fences
    (D) Visiting National Parks

2. Redwood trees are cared for by—
    (A) visitors   (B) forest rangers
    (C) lightning rods   (D) doctors

3. This national park is—
    (A) 500 miles long   (B) 367 feet high
    (C) 1,963 miles wide   (D) being destroyed

4. Many years ago there were—
    (A) no redwoods   (B) more statues
    (C) fewer redwoods   (D) more redwoods

5. The word "discovered" in line three means—
    (A) first seen   (B) cut down
    (C) last seen   (D) planted

Israel Bissell was a man that history forgot. When the 23-year-old patriot got word that the war with the British had started, he began a ride fifteen times longer than that of Paul Revere.

Bissell's first horse soon grew tired. With fresh mounts supplied by farmers along the way, Bissell crossed Massachusetts. Though he was asked to *alert* the countryside only as far as Connecticut, Bissell continued on until he arrived in Philadelphia. There he delivered the news of war to City Hall.

For four days and nights, Israel Bissell had spread the alarm on a 300-mile ride. It was a ride to remember—even though history has forgotten.

1. The best title is—
   (A) From Massachusetts to Philadelphia
   (B) Forget Paul Revere
   (C) Riding Horses
   (D) The Ride of Israel Bissell

2. The story says that Bissell's first horse—
   (A) was slow   (B) grew tired
   (C) was fast   (D) became ill

3. Bissell rode—
   (A) 100 miles   (B) 300 miles
   (C) 15 miles   (D) 23 miles

4. You can tell that Bissell could *not* have made the ride without—
   (A) Paul Revere   (B) British help
   (C) the help of farmers   (D) a knowledge of history

5. The word "alert" in line six means—
   (A) see   (B) leave
   (C) warn   (D) farm

Have you ever wrapped something wet in a newspaper? The water comes through the paper and the paper gets *soggy*. It can really be messy.

That is what used to happen to a candlestick maker over ninety years ago. Many nights after work, he would stop and buy fish to take home. The fish would be wrapped in ordinary paper. What a mess! Then he had an idea. Before leaving work, he dipped a piece of paper into the wax he used to make candles. That night he had fish wrapped in the paper with wax on it. The water didn't soak through.

This is how wax paper was invented. Today, we use it for many purposes.

---

1. The best title is—
    (A) A Candlestick Maker
    (B) Fish Can Be Messy
    (C) The First Wax Paper
    (D) Using Wax for Candles

2. If wet fish are wrapped in ordinary paper, the paper—
    (A) falls apart   (B) stays dry
    (C) stays neat   (D) soaks through

3. The man who invented wax paper—
    (A) made wax   (B) made candles
    (C) sold fish   (D) sold paper

4. The candlestick maker in the story was—
    (A) hard working   (B) old
    (C) young   (D) clever

5. The word "soggy" in line two means—
    (A) dry   (B) wet
    (C) light   (D) heavy

A. Exercising Your Skill

In Unit 16, you learned that the word *motel* comes from blending, or putting together, the words *motor* and *hotel*. Other words like *motel* have been created in interesting ways. Read this passage.

Most people believe that English began around the fifth century. At that time, three tribes invaded England. They spoke a language called Anglo-Saxon. That language was very different from the English spoken today. In fact, to us Anglo-Saxon would sound like a foreign language! The reason for this is simple. Over the centuries, English has changed greatly.

Even today English is changing. Words are always being added to the language. Many of these words come to us in unusual ways. For example, some words like *motel* and *smog* are a blend of two words. *Smog* is a blend of *smoke* and *fog*. Other words are formed by joining two words together. *Birth* and *day* have been joined to make *birthday*. Still other words are formed by making long words shorter. *Advertisement*, for example, has been shortened to *ad*.

Decide what words below were formed (1) by blending two words, (2) by joining two words, and (3) by making a long word short. Then, on your own paper, write the word(s) the new words came from.

1. sunglasses = _____
2. moonlight = _____
3. brunch = _____
4. cab = _____
5. sub = _____

B. Expanding Your Skill

Can you think of any other words that have been formed (1) by blending two words, (2) by joining two words, or (3) by making a long word short? Make three columns on a piece of paper. Write one of these headings at the top of each column: Blending, Joining, and Shortening. Then write as many words under each column as you can. To help you think of words, look in the dictionary.

C. Exploring Language

In the following box are words formed by blending, joining, and shortening. On a piece of paper, write one sentence for each word. Try to show the meaning of each word in your sentence.

> television + broadcast = telecast
> twist + whirl = twirl
> week + end = weekend
> rain + coat = raincoat
> air + plane = airplane

D. Expressing Yourself

Choose one of these activities.

1. Names of some people have also become words. For example, the man who invented the Ferris wheel was named George Ferris. Think about what product you would like to put your name on. Then write a paragraph that describes your choice and your reasons for it.

2. Many words have been borrowed from other languages. For example, did you know that *moccasin* and *raccoon* were borrowed from Native American languages? Look at the first or last line of a dictionary entry. There you will usually find the history of the word. Look up the following words in the dictionary. On a piece of paper, write the language each word was borrowed from. Then write the word as it was written in the original language.

noodle	menu	skunk	chef
volcano	taco	rodeo	hamburger
opera	waltz	waffle	fiesta

Which group of dogs lives in its own town? The answer to this riddle is prairie dogs. However, the question, as in most riddles, is *misleading*. To understand the prairie dog, you need some facts.

For one thing, prairie dogs are not dogs but rodents. That is, they belong to the same family as squirrels and mice. Second, the "towns" are actually connected underground tunnels, or burrows. Years ago, some of these so-called "towns" of the Great Plains in which black-tailed prairie dogs lived, extended many miles and included thousands of these animals.

Prairie dogs were named for their barking voices, or cries. They can still be found in prairies, or grasslands, in the western United States and in northern Mexico.

1. The best title is—
   (A) Towns of the Great Plains
   (B) What Rodents Are Like
   (C) American and Mexican Dogs
   (D) The Facts About Prairie Dogs

2. Prairie dogs are really—
   (A) grasshoppers   (B) rodents
   (C) dogs   (D) poodles

3. The story says that prairie dog towns are really—
   (A) underground burrows   (B) ant colonies
   (C) cities   (D) in the Great Lakes

4. When it comes to building homes, prairie dogs are—
   (A) log splitters   (B) poor diggers
   (C) good diggers   (D) good barkers

5. The word "misleading" in line three means—
   (A) direct   (B) amusing
   (C) confusing   (D) truthful

Some say a caboose looks like a "playhouse on wheels." It has been called a "cabin car," an "office," a "monkeyhouse," and even a conductor's "crummy." The last nickname comes from the fact that early cabooses were often uncomfortable, dangerous, and smelled of coal smoke. Yet many train crews are sad that, instead of being used, more and more cabooses are *idle,* kept in storage around the country.

The caboose was once the command post for the conductor. From the back of the train, the crew in the caboose could spot certain kinds of dangers. Now computers have taken over this important task. No one would have imagined a century ago that the caboose would come to the end of the line—once and for all.

1. The best title is—
   (A) New Uses for Computers
   (B) Houses for Train Crews
   (C) End of the Line for Cabooses
   (D) Riding the Rails

2. One of the workers in the caboose was the—
   (A) passenger   (B) monkey
   (C) conductor   (D) engineer

3. Many cabooses have been replaced by—
   (A) computers   (B) modern headlights
   (C) train crews   (D) engines

4. You know that a caboose is—
   (A) a bus   (B) a train track
   (C) an automobile   (D) a train car

5. The word "idle" in line six means—
   (A) hard at work   (B) bored
   (C) out of work   (D) active

We have all heard many loud noises, but perhaps the loudest noise ever heard was the eruption of a volcano. The volcano was on the island of Krakatoa. It had been *dormant* for two hundred years. Then, in 1883, it erupted and destroyed half the island. The noise was heard in Australia, two thousand miles away. The cinders and ash from the volcano shot twenty miles high, causing darkness one hundred miles around.

The tidal waves that came after the eruption were even worse. These were giant waves caused by the eruption. The waves were one hundred feet high and rushed forward at speeds of seven hundred miles per hour.

Let's hope that we never have another noise as loud as the volcano on Krakatoa.

---

1. The best title is—
   (A) The Eruption on Krakatoa
   (B) Listening for Noises
   (C) Cinders and Ash Fly High
   (D) Huge Tidal Waves

2. The eruption of the volcano was heard—
   (A) 5,000 miles away   (B) 2,000 miles away
   (C) by everyone   (D) by no one

3. Krakatoa is—
   (A) a person   (B) a mountain
   (C) an island   (D) a story

4. The tidal waves probably caused—
   (A) little harm   (B) other eruptions
   (C) many deaths   (D) a few deaths

5. The word "dormant" in line three means—
   (A) causing harm   (B) loud
   (C) causing darkness   (D) quiet

A person's best friend may be a dog, as the saying goes, but did you ever hear of a dog's best friend turning out to be a talent scout?

The talent scout was at a dog pound the night before a dog named Sandy was to be "put to sleep" forever. The scout was searching for any real dog that looked just like the dog in the cartoon "Little Orphan Annie." This dog would appear in the Broadway musical show *Annie*.

The comic-strip dog was famous for its yellowish-red hair. In addition, the cartoon dog always said "Arf." The talent scout noticed that Sandy looked just like the dog in the cartoon. Of course, Sandy didn't have to *rehearse* saying "Arf." The scout quickly paid eight dollars for Sandy and put the animal in the Broadway show. Lucky dog!

1. The best title is—
   (A) A Dog's Life at the Pound
   (B) A Person's Best Friend
   (C) Rescued by a Talent Scout
   (D) A Cartoon About a Dog

2. At the dog pound, Sandy was to be—
   (A) given to an orphan   (B) "put to sleep"
   (C) let go free   (D) given eight dollars

3. Sandy went from a dog pound to—
   (A) a cartoon   (B) a TV program
   (C) a musical show   (D) the park

4. You can tell that Sandy's hair was—
   (A) black   (B) yellowish-red
   (C) wiry   (D) light gray

5. The word "rehearse" in line eleven means—
   (A) practice   (B) forget
   (C) hear   (D) imagine

Many people enjoy the thrill of jumping from an airplane or helicopter. Some jumpers take lessons in jumping as a sport or hobby. Others are trained in the armed forces. Army paratroopers learn how to land in battle areas by parachuting from airplanes. Still other jumpers are specially trained as firefighters.

Just how fast can a person fall before the parachute is opened? It will never be faster than about 130 miles per hour, unless there are high winds. This speed won't change whether the jumper falls one mile or ten miles before opening the chute. When *bailing out* of planes that are very high, jumpers purposely fall a long distance before pulling the release cords of their parachutes. They want to escape as fast as possible from the cold temperature up there!

---

1. The best title is—
   (A) Army Paratroopers
   (B) A Dangerous Sport
   (C) Jumping from an Airplane
   (D) Opening Parachutes

2. The story says that some parachute jumpers are trained to—
   (A) save ships   (B) start fires
   (C) fight fires   (D) be afraid

3. To open a parachute, you pull the—
   (A) release cord   (B) sport cord
   (C) chute cord   (D) jumper button

4. As you go higher, it gets—
   (A) darker   (B) warmer
   (C) colder   (D) funnier

5. The words "bailing out" in line nine mean—
   (A) flying at high altitudes   (B) jumping out with a
                                       parachute
   (C) looking   (D) walking

Morris Frank was unhappy. He had lost his sight. He was *especially* sad because he couldn't go out of the house without having someone help him.

One day Morris heard something that gave him hope. People were training dogs in Europe to guide people that could not see. Morris took the long trip to Europe. He went to the school that taught dogs how to be guide dogs. Morris had things to learn too.

When Morris came home to Morristown, New Jersey, he brought the first Seeing Eye dog to America. The dog's name was Buddy. Then Morris helped to start a school to teach people and their guide dogs to live and work together.

---

1. The best title is—
   (A) Buddy—A Good Dog
   (B) Morris Frank and Seeing Eye Dogs
   (C) Morris Frank Comes Home
   (D) Traveling in Europe

2. The first Seeing Eye dog brought to America was named—
   (A) Morris   (B) Jackie
   (C) Buddy   (D) Frank

3. The first Seeing Eye dog in America came from—
   (A) Morristown   (B) the United States
   (C) Europe   (D) New Jersey

4. The story suggests that Morris Frank and Buddy—
   (A) didn't like each other   (B) got along well
   (C) didn't meet   (D) went back to Europe

5. The word "especially" in line one means—
   (A) very much   (B) very little
   (C) not quite   (D) very seldom

Most people have heard of white bread, rye bread, and even pumpernickel bread—but have you ever heard of monkey bread?

Monkey bread grows on the baobab tree in Africa. It is really a fruit, but it is shaped like a loaf of bread.

The baobab tree is as interesting as its "bread." Its trunk can be thirty feet wide and almost sixty feet high. If the trunk is *hollow*, the space can be used for a home or even a jail. The tree's leaves and bark are used for clothing, paper, rope, and medicine.

The next time you eat a sandwich, think of the useful baobab tree and its unusual monkey bread.

---

1. The best title is—
   (A) Monkeys in Trees
   (B) Five Kinds of Bread
   (C) Monkey Bread and the Baobab Tree
   (D) Hollow Trunks that Serve as Jails

2. Monkey bread is really—
   (A) rye bread   (B) white bread
   (C) pumpernickel bread   (D) a fruit

3. The story says that the baobab tree has—
   (A) two trunks   (B) large roots
   (C) leaves   (D) nuts

4. The people of Africa must think of the baobab tree as—
   (A) troublesome   (B) ugly
   (C) valuable   (D) frightening

5. The word "hollow" in line six means—
   (A) empty   (B) small
   (C) closed   (D) full

What are some of the animals that live in Canada? To find out, you need only look at Canada's money. When the nation became one hundred years old in 1967, it decided to honor its animals by putting their pictures on some of its coins and bills. The animals pictured have changed over the years.

In more recent years, the Canadian coin dollar shows a bird called a loon. An elk with big antlers is on the twenty-five-cent coin. A beaver is on the nickel. You will find a robin on the Canadian two-dollar bill and a bird called the kingfisher on the five-dollar bill.

Putting these animals on money *illustrates* how much the Canadians value them.

1. The best title is—
    (A) Making Coins in Canada
    (B) The Beaver and the Nickel
    (C) Canada—One Hundred Years Old
    (D) Honoring the Animals of Canada

2. The loon is on the—
    (A) two-dollar bill   (B) coin dollar
    (C) nickel   (D) five-dollar bill

3. On the twenty-five-cent coin is an—
    (A) ostrich   (B) eagle
    (C) elk   (D) insect

4. You can tell that Canadians—
    (A) love hunting   (B) respect wildlife
    (C) are wealthy   (D) fear wildlife

5. The word "illustrates" in line ten means—
    (A) hides   (B) saves
    (C) shows   (D) spends

"Don't start forest fires!" Pictures of Smokey the bear have been seen nearly everywhere *advising* us to be careful of matches and fires in forests. His posters tell us to protect our trees and wild animals.

Did you know that Smokey was a real bear? In 1950, there was a terrible fire in New Mexico. A small cub was badly burned and almost died. When he got well, he was named "Smokey" and sent to live in the National Zoo in Washington, D.C. He became the symbol for fire prevention.

At the zoo Smokey received about 200,000 letters a year. Until his recent death he was the most popular bear in the world!

---

1. The best title is—
   (A) Preventing Forest Fires
   (B) Pictures of Smokey
   (C) Smokey—A Real Bear
   (D) Living in a Zoo

2. Smokey was sent to live in—
   (A) New Mexico   (B) a forest
   (C) a zoo   (D) a tree

3. Smokey's posters tell people to—
   (A) be careless   (B) prevent fires
   (C) start fires   (D) visit parks

4. When Smokey was getting well from his burns, he probably—
   (A) was very old   (B) had poor care
   (C) learned to talk   (D) had good care

5. The word "advising" in line two means—
   (A) hoping   (B) telling
   (C) seeing   (D) drawing

The Pony Express lasted for only eighteen months. Still, it is a famous *chapter* in American history. It is famous because of the daring and bravery of its riders.

The Pony Express was started to give faster mail service. The riders were each given a gun, a knife, and a Bible. With only these, they had to brave bad weather, attacks by outlaws, and dangerous trails. They would ride Indian ponies as fast as they could for fifteen miles. Then they would jump off with the mail sack, mount another pony, and be riding again in less than two minutes.

Only the bravest and best riders could work for the Pony Express.

---

1. The best title is—
   - (A) Bad Weather and Outlaw Attacks
   - (B) Indian Ponies Deliver Mail
   - (C) The Pony Express
   - (D) Brave Riders and Their Horses

2. The Pony Express lasted for—
   - (A) eighteen months
   - (B) two years
   - (C) twenty days
   - (D) two minutes

3. One danger mentioned in the story was—
   - (A) tornadoes
   - (B) deserts
   - (C) bad weather
   - (C) landslides

4. Each pony was ridden for only fifteen miles because—
   - (A) it would get lost
   - (B) the rider wanted a change
   - (C) it became tired
   - (D) it needed a bath

5. The word "chapter" in line two means—
   - (A) book
   - (B) poem
   - (C) whole
   - (D) part

Silver was once used mostly for money and for making jewelry. Today it is even more valuable because it has many more uses. It is one of the most important metals we have.

Silver is used in electric toasters, batteries, rockets, and medicine. It is used to fill teeth, destroy warts, and sew broken bones. It is even used in film for cameras. In India, some people have a *strange* use for silver. They make thin sheets of the metal and wrap it around fruit. Then they eat both the fruit and the silver! They believe it improves their health.

Silver is certainly one of our most valuable metals.

---

1. The best title is—
   (A) Sewing Bones with Silver
   (B) A Strange Way to Eat Fruit
   (C) Silver—An Important Metal
   (D) Money and Jewelry

2. Silver has—
   (A) few uses   (B) no use
   (C) one use   (D) many uses

3. Silver is used to—
   (A) fill bones   (B) destroy teeth
   (C) fill teeth   (D) make roads

4. Today we need—
   (A) more silver than before   (B) more fruit
   (C) less silver than before   (D) more jewelry

5. The word "strange" in line six means—
   (A) common   (B) unusual
   (C) sad   (D) famous

Buses, trains, and airplanes are all common ways to travel. In San Francisco there is an unusual way to travel. It is the world-famous cable car. For over one hundred years, cable cars have carried people up and down the steep hills of San Francisco.

The cable cars are made of steel and wood. A cable, which is a rope made of twisted wires, runs just beneath the surface of the road. It is always moving. When the cable cars are about to go, they *attach* themselves to the moving cable. When they are about to stop, they let go of the cable and put on their brakes.

Visitors and people who live in San Francisco love to ride the cable cars.

---

1. The best title is—
   (A) Cable Cars
   (B) The Hills of San Francisco
   (C) Different Ways to Travel
   (D) A Dangerous Ride

2. Cable cars are made of—
   (A) all wood   (B) all steel
   (C) wires   (D) wood and steel

3. The cable that pulls cable cars is—
   (A) made of wood   (B) made of thread
   (C) beneath the road   (D) above the road

4. In San Francisco, riding the cable cars is—
   (A) the only way to get around   (B) a dangerous way to get around
   (C) a slow way to get around   (D) a fun way to get around

5. The word "attach" in line seven means—
   (A) let go   (B) fasten
   (C) stop   (D) move

It's a common, everyday sight. Many adults—especially men—greet each other by shaking hands. Did you ever wonder how this custom came about?

Think about what it might mean to extend an open hand to someone. Remember, your hand is empty. Do you mean no harm to that person? Handshaking, some experts say, was first done to show good wishes. Long, long ago, when a villager met a stranger who offered his empty hand, the villager could see that the stranger was not holding a weapon. So it was safe to greet that person.

Other experts argue that the handshake first signaled the *transfer* of power. By shaking hands, might people have shown that they were willing to pass along their power to another? The ancient picture word for the Egyptian verb meaning "to give" is that of an outstretched hand.

If they met, would these experts shake hands?

---

1. The best title is—
   (A) Settling Arguments
   (B) Empty-handed
   (C) How the Handshake Came About
   (D) Experts Greet Each Other

2. Some experts say that the first handshake signaled—
   (A) unfriendly feelings   (B) good wishes
   (C) fear   (D) good manners

3. Other experts say that the first handshake showed—
   (A) an exchange of money   (B) a happy meeting
   (C) an exchange of power   (D) an exchange of food

4. When it comes to how the handshake began, experts—
   (A) disagree   (B) have no opinion
   (C) agree   (D) draw pictures

5. The word "transfer" in line ten means—
   (A) hope for   (B) price of
   (C) handing over   (D) holding back

Have you ever heard of a dog who got himself into hot water? A dog named Luke once locked himself in a car—and his owner out!

Luke, it seems, got into the front seat of his owner's car. The five-week-old puppy jumped behind the wheel and somehow hit the button that locked all the doors. Then he turned on the left-turn signal and started the windshield wiper. When Mrs. Stolley, his owner, returned, Luke was honking the horn.

It's a good thing Mrs. Stolley's *spare* set of car keys arrived when it did. Maybe little Luke would have turned the key and driven away!

1. The best title is—
   (A) Luke Looks In
   (B) Honk the Horn
   (C) Luke Gets Locked In
   (D) A Dog Takes a Trip

2. Luke was—
   (A) five years old   (B) three months old
   (C) five weeks old   (D) seven weeks old

3. When Mrs. Stolley returned, Luke was—
   (A) running around   (B) honking the horn
   (C) sitting quietly   (D) barking

4. You can tell that Luke must have been—
   (A) happy   (B) frisky
   (C) sleepy   (D) dreamy

5. The word "spare" in line eight means—
   (A) extra   (B) lost
   (C) heavy   (D) metal

In Unit 32, you read about Canada's decision to put animals on its coins. Because these coins are so beautiful, many people collect them. Have you ever thought about collecting coins? Read this passage. As you read, look for the main idea of the paragraph.

Collecting coins is a great hobby. If it weren't, over five million people today wouldn't be coin collectors. Collecting coins is fun for several reasons. For instance, if you're a coin collector, you're like a detective. You always have to think of new places to find coins. (Have you ever looked through any old clothes in your grandparents' attic?) As a coin collector, you also always have the chance of getting rich. A taxicab driver once found a penny worth $115. In addition, you usually get to meet some very nice people. When you're a coin collector, you should join a coin club. If you do, you'll have lots of people to trade coins with. Most of all, collecting coins gives you a successful feeling when you complete one set of coins. And who knows—in thirty or forty years, you might want to pass on your coin collection to your son or daughter.

A. Exercising Your Skill

On a piece of paper, do the following:

1. Write the one sentence in the paragraph that best states the main idea.
2. Write the main idea of this paragraph in your own words.

B. Expanding Your Skill

In a well-written paragraph, the main idea will have supporting details. These details give more information about the main idea. Copy the following diagram on a piece of paper. Notice that the main idea is in the center. On the lines joined to the center, write some details that support the main idea. One has been done for you.

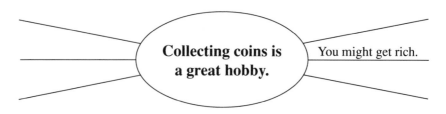

Collecting coins is a great hobby.

You might get rich.

C. Exploring Language

Choose one of the following main idea sentences. Then use it in a paragraph. Remember that the other sentences in your paragraph should include details that support the main idea sentence.

1. You can learn a lot about your country if you collect your country's stamps.
2. Collecting baseball cards is an interesting hobby.
3. Instead of spending time on a hobby, I would rather earn some money.
4. All hobbies are boring and are a waste of time.

D. Expressing Yourself

Choose one of these activities.

1. Write to the American Numismatic Association. (*Numismatics* means "the study and collecting of money.") Ask for more information about collecting coins. Send your letter to the following address.

   American Numismatic Association
   P. O. Box 2366
   Colorado Springs, Colorado 80901

   Share the information you get with your classmates.

2. Write a paragraph that tells about a hobby you have now or that you used to have. Explain how and why you began it. Then tell why you would recommend it to others. Share your hobby with your classmates. If possible, bring to school some items that represent your hobby.

3. Take a survey. Ask your friends and classmates what their favorite hobby is. At the end, count the number of people who liked the different hobbies. Which hobby was the most popular? Which was the least popular? Share what you have learned in an interesting way—on a chart or poster, for example.

Most children today go to a school where each class has its own room. It was different many years ago. Most children went to a one-room schoolhouse. In a one-room schoolhouse all the children learned in one room from the same teacher. A fourth grader might have sat next to a ninth grader. *Possibly* you have seen a one-room schoolhouse on a television program.

There was a good reason for many of the one-room schoolhouses. They were often located in the country, where there were only ten or twenty children going to school. One room was then big enough for everyone! Today there are many more children going to school. The one-room schoolhouse has just about disappeared.

---

1. The best title is—
   (A) Today's Schoolhouses
   (B) The One-room Schoolhouse
   (C) Big Enough for Everyone
   (D) Fourth and Ninth Graders

2. Children going to a one-room schoolhouse had—
   (A) the same teacher   (B) different teachers
   (C) no lunch period   (D) no homework

3. Schoolhouses today usually have—
   (A) one room   (B) one teacher
   (C) twenty pupils   (D) more than one room

4. One-room schoolhouses were *not* used where—
   (A) there were farms nearby   (B) people lived far apart
   (C) there were many pupils   (D) there was one teacher

5. The word "possibly" in line five means—
   (A) sadly   (B) maybe
   (C) luckily   (D) often

The first woman to climb the highest mountain in the world was Japanese. Mrs. Junko Tabei reached the top of Mount Everest on May 16, 1975. Her husband and three-year-old daughter did not go along on the trip.

Fourteen other Japanese women made most of the trip up the mountain. Both Mrs. Tabei and some of the other mountain climbers were badly injured when large amounts of snow and ice fell on their camp. But Mrs. Tabei kept going. After packing only what she needed, she and one guide decided to try for the very top. In spite of bad weather, they *attained* their goal. It had been a long and dangerous trip. Mount Everest is 29,028 feet high!

1. The best title is—
    (A) Mount Everest—The Highest Mountain
    (B) The Dangers of Mountain Climbing
    (C) A Woman and the Highest Mountain
    (D) Chinese Women

2. Climbing Mount Everest was—
    (A) a lot of fun   (B) quite safe
    (C) dangerous   (D) impossible

3. During the climb, Mrs. Tabei was—
    (A) killed   (B) badly hurt
    (C) disappointed   (D) lost in the snow

4. You can tell from the story that Mrs. Tabei had—
    (A) no courage   (B) great courage
    (C) little intelligence   (D) little fear

5. The word "attained" in line ten means—
    (A) changed   (B) missed
    (C) forgot   (D) reached

Many people read the comic strips in daily and Sunday newspapers. Each strip is usually made up of three or four pictures that tell a story. Sometimes a story is *completed* in one strip. In other strips the story continues for years!

One of the first comic strips was "The Yellow Kid," printed in 1896. A little boy wearing bright yellow was the main cartoon character. "The Katzenjammer Kids" came out in 1897, and "Buster Brown" in 1902. Small boys began dressing like Buster Brown. Through the years, comic strips have included stories of animals and people. Many are filled with jokes. One of today's most popular comic strips is "Peanuts." Although they started in America, comic strips are now enjoyed all over the world.

1. The best title is—
   (A) The Yellow Kid
   (B) Animals and People
   (C) Some Famous Comic Strips
   (D) Cartoons and Newspapers

2. The comic strip that began in 1902 was—
   (A) The Yellow Kid
   (B) Peanuts
   (C) Superman
   (D) Buster Brown

3. The story says that comic strips can be seen in—
   (A) magazines
   (B) movies
   (C) newspapers
   (D) comic books

4. The story suggests that comic strips can affect people's—
   (A) clothes
   (B) houses
   (C) pets
   (D) vacations

5. The word "completed" in line three means—
   (A) started
   (B) finished
   (C) colored
   (D) understood

The largest bird that ever lived probably died only a few hundred years ago. It weighed about 1,000 pounds and stood ten feet tall. Its name—the elephant bird—describes it well. Its correct name is *Aepyornis*.

Explorer Luis Marden was always interested in the elephant bird. As a boy, he had read stories about it and dreamed of someday seeing one. Unfortunately, they had all died long before his time. He did the next best thing; he *located* two eggs of the elephant bird. Both were found on the island of Madagascar.

Today, visitors can see one the elephant bird's eggs in National Geographic, Explorers Hall, in Washington, D.C. It is shown next to the egg of a hummingbird—the smallest egg of all.

---

1. The best title is—
   (A) Explorer Luis Marden
   (B) An Elephant's Egg
   (C) A Dream Come True
   (D) The Elephant Bird

2. The elephant bird—
   (A) is still alive
   (B) died 100 years ago
   (C) was 1,000 feet tall
   (D) weighed about 1,000 pounds

3. Madagascar is—
   (A) an island
   (B) a lake
   (C) a bird
   (D) an elephant

4. The world's largest bird was named the elephant bird because of its—
   (A) trunk
   (B) color
   (C) size
   (D) wings

5. The word "located" in line eight means—
   (A) lost
   (B) ate
   (C) found
   (D) cooked

"Kee-i!" The feet of a karate expert fly through the air and *strike* an enemy. The enemy falls.

"Karate" means "empty hands." It developed in China and then traveled to Thailand, Okinawa, and Japan. Long ago in these lands, kings often took all the weapons away from the people. Only the king's soldiers had weapons. The people had to develop a way of fighting, using only their feet, elbows, and hands. It was called karate.

Today, karate is a sport. People all over the world learn it to keep their bodies in good condition. There are even karate contests. Of course, today's experts don't really strike to hurt.

---

1. The best title is—
    (A) The Karate of Japan
    (B) The Story of Karate
    (C) Keeping in Good Condition
    (D) The Sport of Japan

2. Karate began in—
    (A) Japan   (B) China
    (C) Okinawa   (D) Thailand

3. In karate, you do not fight with your—
    (A) knees   (B) hands
    (C) elbows   (D) feet

4. Long ago, people learned karate because—
    (A) their bodies were weak   (B) they had no weapons
    (C) they were strong   (D) they liked contests

5. The word "strike" in line one means—
    (A) brush by   (B) amuse
    (C) hit   (D) frighten

Most animals protect their young until they are old enough to take care of themselves. A fish that swims in the rivers of South America protects its young in a very strange way. This fish, a kind of catfish, uses its mouth to keep its babies from danger.

When this catfish lays its eggs, it carries them in its mouth. From what we know, it does not eat during this time. After the eggs hatch, the fish swims with its young to protect them. It opens its mouth when danger appears, and the tiny fish swim inside. They swim out only when it is safe again.

These catfish may have a *peculiar* way to protect their young, but it seems to work.

---

1. The best title is—
   (A) Staying Away from Danger
   (B) How a Fish Protects Its Young
   (C) Laying Eggs
   (D) A Cat that Swims

2. The catfish in the story live in—
   (A) lakes   (B) the ocean
   (C) rivers   (D) North America

3. The young fish are—
   (A) tiny   (B) large
   (C) yellow and gold   (D) very brave

4. If the young fish were not near parents, they would be—
   (A) safer   (B) in greater danger
   (C) happier   (D) less hungry

5. The word "peculiar" in line ten means—
   (A) common   (B) useless
   (C) odd   (D) dangerous

Can a bird sew? The tailorbird can, of course! This clever bird needs no store-bought sewing needle.

Most birds build nests for their young. Many use mud or sticks. The tailorbird, however, has a special *technique* for making a nest. It actually stitches together a nest of leaves.

With its sharp, pointed beak, this bird punches holes in the edges of two leaves. Next, the tailor bird takes small, strong fibers in its beak and threads them through the holes. As the bird pulls on the fibers, the two leaves are stitched together tightly. Then the busy bird looks for soft grasses to put inside. This makes for a nice, cozy nest.

1. The best title is—
   (A) Building Homes for Birds
   (B) How to Use Leaves
   (C) How a Tailorbird Makes a Nest
   (D) Tailoring for a Living

2. The bird in the story makes a nest from—
   (A) mud   (B) leaves
   (C) sticks   (D) cloth

3. The tailor bird "sews" with its—
   (A) wings   (B) feet
   (C) beak   (D) head

4. The story suggests that birds build their nests—
   (A) the same way   (B) to keep busy
   (C) in different ways   (D) to be friendly

5. The word "technique" in line four means—
   (A) reason   (B) need
   (C) machine   (D) method

In 1986, Paula Enyeart, a 26-year-old registered nurse from North Dakota, was living in a small village in Ecuador. She had been working there for the past three years without pay. Enyeart was a Peace Corps volunteer. She was proud and happy to help. There are thousands of Americans around the world who volunteer their services and who feel the same pride as Enyeart.

Years ago, an *organization* of unpaid traveling helpers made up of American volunteers was just a dream. President John F. Kennedy launched the Peace Corps in 1961 with little more than the hopes and energy of the young and old volunteers who joined it. Over the years, it has gone through changes. Today, the Peace Corps has grown up, but its spirit of giving and caring remains.

1. The best title is—
    (A) Paula Enyeart's Paid Vacation
    (B) Volunteer Agencies
    (C) Americans Around the World
    (D) The Continuing Spirit of the Peace Corps

2. The Peace Corps was founded—
    (A) in 1986   (B) in 1961
    (C) 26 years ago   (D) over the years

3. Members of the Peace Corps are—
    (A) young   (B) volunteers
    (C) old   (D) paid

4. You know that Enyeart probably helped the village in—
    (A) agriculture   (B) learning crafts
    (C) health care   (D) planning trips

5. The word "organization" in line seven means—
    (A) business   (B) gang
    (C) group   (D) class

Do you know what your first name means? If your name is Charles, Carlos, or even Charlotte, your name means "strong." This same meaning applies if your name is Francis or Frances. What if your name is Helen, Ellen, or perhaps Nell? However you spell the name, it means "light." Yes, some names are related.

Since many names have meanings, they should fit the *individuals* they belong to. For example, if you are a lover of horses, you might well be named Philip.

Long ago people had only first names. If someone was called Charles or Helen, that was the only name he or she had. It had to mean something. Today, parents select their children's names for many different reasons. Is your name the right choice for you?

1. The best title is—
   (A) What Names Mean
   (B) A Woman Named Helen
   (C) A Man Named Charles
   (D) Parents and Children

2. The names Helen and Ellen—
   (A) mean "light"   (B) are unrelated
   (C) are last names   (D) mean "strong"

3. The story says that long ago people had—
   (A) only first names   (B) only last names
   (C) no names   (D) first and last names

4. The story suggests that, long ago, the meanings of names were—
   (A) all related   (B) mysterious
   (C) unimportant   (D) very important

5. The word "individuals" in line six means—
   (A) crowds   (B) persons
   (C) objects   (D) families

You may have seen an ice skater cut a figure eight on the ice. Some bees can do this too. No, they don't ice-skate, but they do form the figure eight when they "dance." Some honeybees do this to let other honeybees know where there is food.

A scout bee who has found food in the field returns home to the hive. It tries to *attract* the attention of the other honeybees. This bee makes a series of loops and straight runs. The middle line of the figure eight shows the direction and distance of the source of food. The line is invisible. The angle of the bee's body and the speed with which the bee moves actually signal the information. The worker bees then hurry off to bring back the food.

1. The best title is—
    (A) The Figure Eight
    (B) Food for Thought
    (C) Dance of the Honeybees
    (D) It Figures!

2. Food is found by the—
    (A) worker bee   (B) queen bee
    (C) scout bee   (D) bumblebee

3. The home of the honeybee is a—
    (A) figure eight   (B) plant
    (C) field   (D) hive

4. The story suggests that honeybees are—
    (A) always hungry   (B) well organized
    (C) almost invisible   (D) very independent

5. The word "attract" in line six means—
    (A) confuse   (B) catch
    (C) throw off   (D) forget

UNIT 49

The Curies are an honored family of French scientists. Marie and Pierre Curie are known for their work in radioactivity and radium. Together they won the 1903 Nobel Prize in physics. Marie Curie went on to win an *additional* Nobel Prize in 1911. This time she was on her own. The field she won it in was chemistry. She was the first person to win two Nobel Prizes.

The Curie family's successes did not end there. In 1935, their daughter Irène and her husband Frédéric Joliot received the Nobel Prize in chemistry for their own work in radioactivity!

Does talent run in families? Marie Curie had her own thoughts on the subject. "We must believe," she said, "that we are gifted for something, and that this thing, at whatever cost, must be obtained."

1. The best title is—
   (A) The Nobel Prize
   (B) Marie Curie
   (C) Research in Radioactivity
   (D) A Family of Nobel Prize Winners

2. Marie and Pierre Curie together won the Nobel Prize in—
   (A) chemistry   (B) radioactivity
   (C) physics   (D) biology

3. Marie Curie won a Nobel Prize on her own in—
   (A) 1903   (B) 1935
   (C) 1911   (D) 1901

4. Marie Curie believed that all people—
   (A) should study physics   (B) should use their talents
   (C) have very many talents (D) can receive the Nobel Prize

5. The word "additional" in line four means—
   (A) more important   (B) unimportant
   (C) extra   (D) less important

Most people are married in a church, but when Arno and Ann were married, it was different. They decided to get married in a place where no one had ever been married before. They decided to go to the World's Fair—to the parachute ride. Up into the air they went—the minister, the maid of honor, the best man, the four musicians, and the happy couple.

On August 25, 1940, the marriage took place with all members of the group *suspended* from parachutes. It was the first parachute wedding in history!

1. The best title is—
   (A) Four Musicians
   (B) Married in the Air
   (C) Saved by a Parachute
   (D) The World's Fair

2. Arno and Ann were married—
   (A) in an airplane   (B) in a church
   (C) in the air   (D) when they were young

3. The story says that the wedding took place—
   (A) on a Sunday   (B) during winter
   (C) in August   (D) in the rain

4. Arno and Ann must have—
   (A) been shy   (B) disliked closed spaces
   (C) liked parachute rides   (D) wanted a small wedding

5. The word "suspended" in line eight means—
   (A) dressed   (B) rising
   (C) hanging   (D) singing

A. Exercising Your Skill

In Unit 39, you read a story about one-room schoolhouses. Although the writer did not state this directly, you could tell from the story that today in most places, one-room schoolhouses would not work for today's students. When you read, you often can "read between the lines" and use what you already know to infer certain information. Read this passage about the working conditions of children many years ago.

Around 1900, children were almost like prisoners in mills and factories all along the East Coast. Often they toiled twelve hours a day, six days a week. For their work they received only five or ten cents an hour. Many factories and mills were poorly lit and had little fresh air.

In March 1911, a fire broke out at the Triangle Shirtwaist Factory. The factory was on the eighth floor of an old New York building. When the children and other workers tried to get out, they found that the doors were locked. Everyone rushed around, trying to escape. Some jumped to the ground below; others died in the fire. A total of 146 workers lost their lives that day.

On your paper, write answers to these questions.

1. Which word best describes working conditions around the turn of the century: fair, bad, horrible?
2. What clue word or words from the passage helped you answer question 1?
3. What do you know about working conditions today that also helped you answer question 1?

B. Expanding Your Skill

In the passage about working children, some of the words created bad, or negative, feelings. For example, words such as *prisoners* and *toiled* gave you clues that working conditions were not good. Now read the pairs of words in the box below. On a piece of paper, write the word in each pair that has a more negative feeling to it.

poor — miserable	wet — drenched
starving — hungry	skinny — slim
proud —boastful	smashed — broken

C. Exploring Language

Write a paragraph that describes your very own private space at home. First tell where that space is—such as in a room of your own or a shared room with one or more brothers or sisters. Then include many details. For example, tell what is in the room, how the room is kept, and what sounds or smells are in the room. As you write, however, do not state whether you like your private space or not. When you have finished, trade papers with a partner. After reading each other's descriptions, you each should decide whether or not your partner likes his or her own space. Then discuss what clues helped each of you come to that conclusion.

D. Expressing Yourself

Choose one of these activities.

1. With a partner, make up two little plays. In the first play, you should be two students who like school. In the second play, you should be two students who don't like school. In both plays, however, never come right out and say whether or not you like school. You should, however, carefully plan clues that will help the other students guess if you like or dislike school. After you put on the plays, have the other students point out the clues that helped them draw the right conclusion.

2. Play a word game with a small group of classmates. Each of you should say one of the following words. Then everyone else should take turns giving a similar word that has a bad, or negative, feeling. Often there will be more than one word for each answer. For example, for the word *work*, you could say *struggle, toil, slave,* or *push*. The words, especially the negative ones, may be acted out.

speak	loud	sit	alone
move	walk	take	sharp